FORENSICS
AND MODERN
DISASTERS

WRITTEN BY:
Rebecca Stefoff

YA

mc Marshall Cavendish
Benchmark
New York

All websites were available and accurate when this book was sent to press.

LIBRARY OF CONGRESS CATALOGING-IN-PUBLICATION DATA
Stefoff, Rebecca
Forensics and modern disasters / by Rebecca Stefoff.
p. cm. — (Forensic science investigated)
Includes bibliographical references and index. ISBN 978-0-7614-4144-1
1. Criminal investigation—Juvenile literature. 2. Forensic sciences—Juvenile literature.
3. Disasters—Juvenile literature. 4. Disaster victims—Identification—
Juvenile literature. I. Title.
HV8073.8.S7384 2011   363.34'65—dc22   2010010533

EDITOR: Christina Gardeski   PUBLISHER: Michelle Bisson
ART DIRECTOR: Anahid Hamparian   SERIES DESIGNER: Kristen Branch

Photo Research by Lindsay Aveilhe
Cover photo by Jewel Samad/AFP/Getty Images
The photographs in this book are used with permission and through the courtesy of: David McNew/Getty Images: p. 4; Richard Perry/The New York Times/Redux: p. 11; John Sommers II/Reuters: 12; UPI/Brian Kersey/Newscom: p. 15; AP Photo/Ed Reinke: p. 17; AFP Photo/Peter Muhly/Newscom: p. 21; Science Photo Library/Photo Researchers: p. 23; Matt Nager/Redux: p. 25; Peter Hilz 2008/Redux: p. 27; AP Photo/Lexington Herald-Leaders, David Stephenson: pp. 31, 33; Romeo Gacad/AFP/Getty Images: p. 36; Paul Sancya/AP Photo: p. 39; John Mottern/AFP/Newscom: p. 40; CNN/Getty Images: pp. 42, 44; Reuters/Corbis: p. 46; Darren McCollester/Getty Images: p. 48; Bob Breidenbach-Pool/Getty Images: p. 50; Douglas McFadd/Getty Images; p. 51; Stringer SS/CP/Reuters: p. 55; Arko Datta AD/fa/Reuters: p. 56; Newscom: p. 59; Pornchai Kittiwongsakul/AFP/Getty Images: p. 60; Stuart Franklin/Magnum Photos: p. 61; Newscom: p. 62; Eranga Jayawardena/AP Photo: p. 64; U.S. Navy/Science Faction/Corbis: p. 66; Reuters: p. 69; Richard Drew/AP Photo: p. 73; Peter Turnley/Corbis: p. 74; Reuters/Corbis: p. 78; Dennis Brack/Black Star/Newscom: p. 79; Orjan Ellingvag/Corbis Sygma: p. 83; Tyler Hicks/The New York Times/Redux: p. 84.

Printed in Malaysia (T)
1 3 5 6 4 2

Cover: A tsunami that struck the coast of Aceh, Indonesia, in 2004 left widespread

CONTENTS

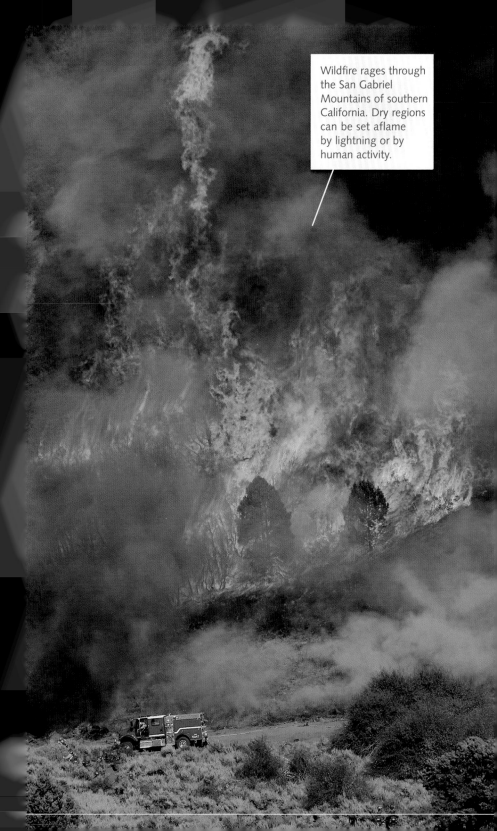

Wildfire rages through the San Gabriel Mountains of southern California. Dry regions can be set aflame by lightning or by human activity.

WHAT IS FORENSICS?

DISASTER STRIKES IN many forms. A bolt of lightning hitting a dry tree can set off a devastating wildfire that devours homes and destroys lives. Terrorists' bombs have exploded in many countries, bringing sudden death to thousands of people. Earthquakes not only tear down homes and smash bridges but sometimes unleash the huge, deadly waves known as tsunamis.

Some disasters are natural events—fires, earthquakes, floods, tornadoes, hurricanes, blizzards, and more. Other disasters have human origins. Accidents such as airplane crashes involve human activities or technology, while bombings and terrorist attacks are deliberate. The term "disaster" fits all these events, and many others. Any sudden happening that causes mass deaths, injuries, or property damage can be called a disaster.

In every disaster, saving lives is the first priority of the firefighters, doctors, and other emergency workers on the scene. After these first responders have rescued every survivor, however, they face other challenges. They must recover and identify the remains of those who have died, if possible. At the same time, in the case of disasters that might have involved deliberate acts, such as arson or bombing, investigators must find out what happened, and who was to blame, with the goal of bringing the criminals to justice. Forensic scientists play a leading role in recovering and identifying the victims of disasters. They also play a role in disaster investigation.

Forensic science is the use of scientific methods and tools to investigate crimes and bring suspects to trial. The term "forensic" comes from ancient Rome, where people debated matters of law in a public meeting place called the Forum. The Latin word *forum* gave rise to *forensic*, meaning "relating to courts of law or to public debate."

Today the term "**forensics**" has several meanings. One is the art of speaking in debates, which is why some schools have forensics clubs or teams for students who want to learn debating skills. The best-known meaning of "forensics," though, is crime solving through forensic science.

Fascination with forensics explains the popularity of many TV shows, movies, and books, but crime and science have been linked for a long time. The first science used in criminal investigation was medicine, and one of the earliest reports of forensic medicine comes from ancient Rome. In 44 BCE, the Roman leader Julius Caesar was stabbed to death not far from the Forum. A physician named Antistius examined the body and found that Caesar had received twenty-three stab wounds, but only one wound was fatal.

Antistius had performed one of history's first recorded **postmortem** examinations, in which a physician looks at a body to find out how the person died. But forensics has always had limits. Antistius could point out the chest wound that had killed Caesar, but he could not say who had struck the deadly blow.

Death in its many forms inspired the first forensic manuals. The oldest one was published in China in 1248. Called *Hsi duan yu* (The Washing Away of Wrongs), it tells how the bodies of people who have been strangled differ from drowning victims. When a corpse is recovered from the water, says the manual, officers of the law should examine the tissues and small bones in the neck. Torn tissues and broken bones show that the victim met with foul play before being thrown into the water.

Poison became another landmark in the history of forensics in 1813, when Mathieu Orfila, a professor of medical and forensic chemistry at the University of Paris, published *Traité des poisons* (A Treatise on

Poisons). Orfila described the deadly effects of various mineral, vegetable, and animal substances. He laid the foundation of the modern science of toxicology, the branch of forensics that deals with poisons, drugs, and their effects on the human body.

As France's most famous expert on poisons, Orfila played a part in an 1840 criminal trial that received wide publicity. A widow named Marie LaFarge was accused of murdering her husband. Orfila, who had examined the man's corpse, testified that he had found arsenic in the stomach. LaFarge insisted that she had not fed the arsenic to her husband, and that therefore he must have eaten it while away from home. The court, however, sentenced her to life imprisonment. Pardoned in 1850 after ten years in prison, LaFarge died the next year, claiming innocence to the end.

Cases such as the LaFarge trial highlighted the growing use of medical evidence in criminal investigations and trials. Courts were recognizing other kinds of forensic evidence, too. In 1784 a British murder case had been decided by physical evidence. The torn edge of a piece of newspaper found in the pocket of a suspect named John Toms matched the torn edge of a ball of paper found in the wound of a man who had been killed by a pistol shot to the head (at the time people used rolled pieces of cloth or paper, called wadding, to hold bullets firmly in gun barrels). Toms was declared guilty of murder. In 1835, an officer of Scotland Yard, Britain's famous police division, caught a murderer by using a flaw on the fatal bullet to trace the bullet to its maker. Such cases marked the birth of ballistics, the branch of forensics that deals with firearms.

Not all forensic developments involved murder. Science also helped solve crimes such as arson and forgery. By the early nineteenth century, chemists had developed the first tests to identify certain dyes used in ink. Experts could then determine the age and chemical makeup of the ink on documents, such as wills and valuable manuscripts, that were suspected of being fakes.

Forensics started to become a regular part of police work at the end of the nineteenth century, after an Austrian law professor named Hans Gross published a two-volume handbook on the subject in 1893. Gross's book, usually referred to as *Criminal Investigation*, brought together all the many techniques that scientists and law enforcers had developed for examining the physical evidence of crime—bloodstains, bullets, and more. Police departments started using *Criminal Investigation* to train officers. The book entered law school courses as well.

Modern forensics specialists regard Hans Gross as the founder of their profession. Among other contributions, Gross invented the word "criminalistics." He used it to refer to the general study of crime or criminals.

Today, however, criminalistics has a narrower, more specific meaning. It refers to the study of physical evidence from crime scenes. "Forensics" is a more general term that covers a broader range of investigative techniques and activities, including identifying unknown crime victims—or disaster victims.

After a disaster, the teams that recover victims' bodies and investigate the causes of the event may include men and women from many branches of forensic science. Following the terrorist attacks on the United States in September 2001, for example, hundreds of experts worked for days, weeks, even years to answer questions about the tragic events of 9/11. Many of them were volunteers who risked their own health and safety to sift through the hazardous debris left by the explosions in New York City and Washington, D.C. These experts came from many medical and scientific fields. Their areas of special knowledge ranged from **DNA** analysis, which is the study of human genetic material, to **metallurgy**, the science of metals and how they behave. Like the other events described in this book, 9/11 showed the vital role of forensics in the aftermath of a large-scale calamity.

Whether a disaster is a natural event, an accident, or a criminal act, it may do much more than kill people and destroy property. A major disaster can weaken the economy or shatter the well-being of a community, a

▲ New York City firefighters carry a fallen colleague from the ruins of the World Trade Center, where hundreds of police officers and firefighters perished on 9/11.

region, or a nation. Disasters affect individual lives, too. In addition to the financial and practical problems of cleaning up and rebuilding, survivors often struggle with emotional and psychological aftereffects. Forensic investigation does not solve these problems. Yet by identifying remains, however badly damaged, forensic investigation gives victims' mourning families and friends some closure. Forensic investigators can also help us understand what happened in a disaster—and that, in turn, may help us prevent future disasters, or limit the damage that they do.

Coroners' vans depart the scene of an airplane crash on a Kentucky hillside. All but one of the people aboard the aircraft died in the accident.

CHAPTER ONE

WHEN CATASTROPHE STRIKES

▼ EARLY ON A SUNDAY MORNING IN

August 2006, a commuter airplane carrying fifty people taxied onto an airport runway in Lexington, Kentucky. Comair Flight 5191 was preparing to take off. The airport's traffic controllers had directed the plane to a 7,000-foot runway, but neither the traffic controllers nor the plane's crew realized that the plane had turned onto a different runway—one that was only half the desired length.

Flight 5191 began to take off but ran out of runway before it could become airborne. The plane's tail dragged along the ground as the pilot turned the aircraft's nose sharply upward, trying to clear the 8-foot fence at the end of the runway. The landing gear beneath the plane struck the fence, and then the plane hit a cluster of trees. The tail assembly broke away from the fuselage, the main body of the aircraft. Seconds later the plane crashed into a hillside and exploded, less than a thousand feet from the end of the runway. Forty-nine of the people aboard died.

First on the scene were firefighters and other emergency responders. Within a short time the forensic team members began to arrive. The complete Flight 5191 forensic team would consist of about three dozen experts with a variety of backgrounds and responsibilities. To understand their roles, it helps to know who's who in disaster response.

▶ FIRST RESPONDERS

The first people to respond to a disaster often are those who provide emergency services. Depending upon the location and circumstances, they may be firefighters, police or sheriff's deputies, emergency medical technicians (EMTs) in ambulances, military personnel such as members of the National Guard or the Coast Guard, or some combination of these.

Most disaster sites are chaotic and horrifying. The sudden violent interruption of everyday life creates scenes of mass confusion. After Hurricane Katrina flooded the city of New Orleans in 2005, for example, entire neighborhoods were wiped off the map, and the

▲ The first step of emergency responders at any disaster site— such as this airplane crash in a river—is to sift the wreckage for survivors.

streets were clogged with fallen trees and the wreckage of houses. Rescue workers found parts of the city almost unrecognizable and extremely hard to navigate. Explosions such as the collapse of the Twin Towers at New York City's World Trade Center (WTC) on 9/11 cause a different kind of chaos, filling the air with smoke, as well as ash that later blankets the ground. Fragments of material shoot like missiles across a wide area. Explosive volcanic eruptions, such as the 1980 eruption of Mount Saint Helens in Washington State, create similar hazardous conditions.

After any disaster, bodies and body parts may lie scattered around the site. Survivors, who are likely to be injured or in shock, will urgently need rescue and medical care. And even after the initial disaster is over, the site can remain highly dangerous. Smoldering fires, downed power lines, unexploded bombs or gas tanks, buildings or bridges that are structurally weakened or partially destroyed—all these pose dangers for the emergency responders.

PRIORITIES

People who work in emergency services generally receive training in how to respond to a disaster or crisis. Having a clear checklist of priorities helps them avoid confusion and panic. It also allows individuals from different organizations to work together effectively.

The highest priority, always, is saving lives. An emergency responder's first concern on arriving at the site of a disaster is rescuing survivors. This may mean something as basic as immediately leading people away from the scene. Often, though, it is more complicated. Stretchers and other gear may be needed to evacuate the injured. After some types of disasters, such as earthquakes and sinking ships, rescuers search for days or even weeks for survivors who may be trapped or lost. Rescue operations may have to be carried out in the midst of active firefighting or other efforts to prevent further casualties.

Once survivors have been removed from danger and are receiving the medical attention they need, emergency responders concentrate on controlling the disaster scene. If anything can be done to prevent further loss of life or property damage, they do it. This phase of the disaster response could involve fighting a fire, disarming a bomb (a task for specially trained explosives experts), or simply keeping crowds and curiosity seekers away from a flooding river, derailed train, crashed plane, mudslide, or other risky setting.

▲ Crime scene tape encloses the Comair Flight 5191 crash site. A law enforcement officer on patrol keeps both bystanders and the evidence safe.

ORDER AT THE SCENE

First responders are not the only people who have a role to play in disasters. Depending on the size and severity of the disaster, others will become involved in the activity at the disaster scene. These may include forensic professionals, such as criminalists and experts with specialized scientific knowledge, or workers with aid agencies such as the Red Cross. Ordinary citizens may also be involved. They may volunteer, for example, to help search for a missing person or pile sandbags along the banks of a flooding river.

Coordinating the work of everyone at the scene is a major challenge of disaster response. If people from different agencies—firefighters and police officers, for example, or aid workers and the National Guard—are to work together effectively, they must know whose orders to follow. Many nations have created plans for what each level of law enforcement or emergency response should do in a disaster or an emergency. In the United States, most local and state agencies and all federal agencies are trained to use the Incident Command System (ICS), a plan that is designed to make certain that everyone at the scene of a disaster knows who is in charge.

Under the Incident Command System, the first official responder to the scene of an accident or disaster takes command of the scene and remains in control until someone with a higher rank arrives. That means that if firefighters are the first to arrive, the senior firefighter in the crew is the first incident commander. If the first responders on the scene are representatives of law enforcement, the senior police officer or sheriff's deputy takes overall command initially.

The incident commander does not issue orders to everyone on the scene, however. He or she communicates with a senior representative of each group, and that representative heads the chain of command within that individual's group. For example, if the incident commander is a police officer and there are firefighters on the scene, the incident commander will coordinate efforts with the senior firefighter, who will direct the activities of the other firefighters.

Depending on the size of the response team, the incident commander may appoint people to perform special tasks, such as communicating with the media, obtaining supplies, and supervising volunteers. In general, state authorities outrank local officials. When representatives of state agencies arrive at a disaster scene, they usually take over leadership from local agencies. In the same way, federal authorities outrank state officials. The top authority at a large-scale disaster site is generally a representative of the Department of Homeland Security (DHS). The DHS manages disaster or emergency sites according to a plan called the National Response

Framework, which outlines how the federal government interacts with disaster relief workers at all levels.

▶ FORENSIC PROFESSIONALS

For some kinds of disasters, such as plane crashes, explosions, or fires, investigators will eventually have to study the evidence found at the scene to find out what caused the disaster. To prevent evidence from being moved, contaminated by casual handling, or even looted by souvenir hunters, police or other authorities may secure the site with fencing, guards, or both.

Forensic professionals survey the site as soon as it is safe to do so, documenting what they see with photographs and measurements, and collecting evidence. This work may be done by members of police or sheriff's departments who have received some training in how to handle evidence. Or it may be done by evidence technicians, who are trained to gather evidence but not necessarily to analyze it, or by criminalists, who analyze forensic evidence.

Disasters often call for specialists in certain kinds of forensic analysis. Evidence from a fire, for example, is reviewed by someone who is trained to detect signs of arson, the malicious setting of fires. An airplane crash is studied by experts with special knowledge of aircraft construction, materials, and behavior. And after a terrorist bombing, explosives experts study the

▲ Police specialists prepare to collect evidence at the site of a 2010 car bombing in Northern Ireland. Human-caused disasters require forensic investigation.

wreckage, looking for bits of the bomb and mapping the damage. What they learn about the bomb may provide clues about where it was made, and by whom.

CORONERS, MEDICAL EXAMINERS, AND PATHOLOGISTS

Most disasters take lives. A big part of disaster response is recovering the victims' remains and determining how each person died. **Coroners, medical examiners (MEs)**, and **pathologists** perform these tasks after disasters, just as they do in murder cases or other investigations that involve deaths.

Coroners and medical examiners are public officials who serve at the municipal, county, or state level of local government. In the case of a violent, sudden, or mysterious death, it is the coroner or medical examiner who determines what is called the manner of death. There are only four possibilities: natural death, accident, suicide, and **homicide**. If the manner of death cannot be determined with certainty, however, it may be recorded as "unknown."

A coroner and an ME perform similar roles, but there are a few differences between the two offices. Coroners are often elected, while MEs are usually appointed. And while a coroner may have medical training, he or she does not have to be a physician. A coroner's ruling on the manner of death is often based on reports by other expert investigators.

A medical examiner, on the other hand, must be a qualified physician. Unlike a coroner, an ME may perform forensic examinations of bodies. One such examination is the postmortem exam, in which the clothes and the outside of the body are thoroughly checked for evidence. Another is the **autopsy**, a special type of surgery in which an ME examines the interior of the body and removes organs, such as the brain, in the search for information about how the person died.

Another difference between coroners and medical examiners is that coroners typically go to the scenes of accidents, crimes, or disasters. On the scene they pronounce the victims dead and oversee the recovery of bodies. An ME is less likely to go to a scene but may send a representative called a medicolegal investigator to perform those functions. Some counties have coroners, some have MEs, and some have both.

After a disaster, it is important to learn not just the manner of each victim's death but the specific cause. In the case of the Flight 5191 crash, for example, the manner of all the deaths was accident. Individual deaths, however, could have had different causes, such as injuries from the crash, trauma or smoke inhalation from the explosion, or even a heart attack in the seconds before impact.

▲ A forensic scientist reviews photos of a line-up of suspects and a mite bite found on a body. A similar bite on one of the suspects might link that man to the victim.

Forensic anthropologists have helped solve thousands of criminal cases around the world. They have also identified the remains of U.S. service people who died on duty and the victims of human-rights violations such as genocides, found in mass graves around the world.

ODONTOLOGY

Odontology is concerned with the structure, growth, and diseases of teeth. Forensic odontology uses distinctive features of the teeth and jaws to identify individuals, usually by comparing the dead person's teeth with dental records that were made while the person was alive.

DNA ANALYSIS

DNA analysis uses genetic material to identify the unknown dead. DNA, or deoxyribonucleic acid, is present in every cell of the body. It contains the genes that pass inherited features from one generation to the next.

A cell's DNA is a set of molecules arranged in two spiral strands that are connected by shorter sections, like the rungs of a ladder. Each rung consists of two molecules, which form what is called a base pair. The sequence, or series, of base pairs that contains the code for making a specific protein is called a gene. Within each cell, long strands of genes are packed into bundles known as chromosomes. All human cells share the same basic arrangement of DNA, and this pattern is called the human genome. Each individual, however, has his or her own unique arrangement of genes within that genome. For example, the human genome includes instructions for making eyes, but the color of any one person's eyes depends on the specific combination of genetic material that he or she inherited from both parents.

The process of producing a DNA profile that represents a person's unique genetic code is usually called **DNA typing**.

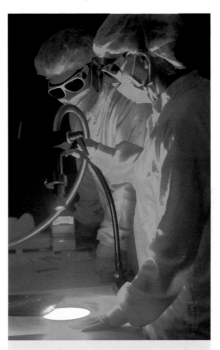

▲ DNA technicians look for trace evidence at the Dutch Forensic Institute in the Netherlands.

Typing is done by removing sections of DNA strands from cells and "mapping" them. The source of the DNA sample can be the root of a hair, skin and tissue cells, blood, saliva, body fluids, or bone tissue. The amount of DNA in any sample is extremely small, but a scientific technique called the polymerase chain reaction (PCR) lets scientists copy the DNA millions of times without altering it. This results in a sample that is large enough to be useful.

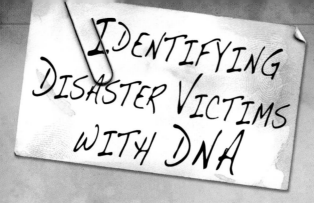

BECAUSE DNA IS UNIQUE to each individual, it can serve in the identification of human remains, but there are limits to its usefulness. Remains that have been burned at very high heat, such as severely charred bone, may not yield DNA that can be analyzed. Exposure to some chemicals can degrade DNA, or change it so much that it becomes unreliable as an identifier. If the only remains available are extremely tiny fragments of bone or tissue, they may not yield enough usable DNA for accurate analysis.

Another problem is that DNA typing can establish a disaster victim's identity *only* if DNA from the victim's remains can be matched to a known DNA sequence. DNA records of criminals and military personnel are stored in databases, but most people have not had their DNA tested. Some forensic and law enforcement professionals believe that the government should collect DNA samples from all citizens and maintain a universal DNA database. Such a collection of samples would make it possible to identify all human remains, as well as to make positive identifications of lost children and people who have lost their memories.

Not everyone agrees that a national DNA database is a good idea, however. Some people feel that the government would be unnecessarily invading people's privacy by storing their genetic information. There may be a risk that insurance companies, government health care programs, or employers would use the information to discriminate against people whose genetic profiles show that they are at higher-than-average risk for certain diseases.

Investigators who are trying to identify genetic material from a disaster site need to compare it with samples of victims' DNA. They look for biological material such as saliva from a victim's toothbrush or hair left in a comb. If no DNA samples from victims are available, investigators will ask for DNA samples from the parents, siblings, or children of victims. These samples are usually collected by means of buccal swabbing—a simple and painless process in which a small wand tipped with cotton is passed with gentle pressure across the inside of the cheek. Although the DNA profiles of close relatives are different from those of the victims themselves, certain relationships exist between the DNA profiles of parents and children. Using a technique called kinship analysis, genetic experts can sometimes prove that a victim was related to someone whose identity is known. But without a possible identity as a starting point, the investigators have nowhere to turn for a sample.

Although DNA typing becomes faster and easier all the time, it is still more expensive and time-consuming than other identification methods. For this reason, disaster recovery teams usually try to identify victims through other methods before turning to DNA typing.

Once it has been multiplied through PCR, the DNA can be typed, or profiled. Analysts focus on parts of the DNA in which short combinations of base pairs repeat over and over on the two parallel strands. These sections are called short tandem repeats, or STRs, and they are different in every person. Currently, DNA analysts and technicians use thirteen specific STR locations, or loci, to create a profile.

▶ DISASTER FORENSICS IN ACTION

Compared with mass disasters such as 9/11 and Hurricane Katrina, the crash of Flight 5191 in Kentucky presented forensic investigators with an uncomplicated case. There was no mystery about what had caused the plane to crash. The disaster site was limited to one hillside, and the remains of all forty-nine victims were concentrated in a small area. Rather than being confronted with hundreds or even thousands of **fatalities** whose identities were unknown, the investigators started with a list of the passengers and crew who had been aboard the plane when it went down.

Yet the tragedy of Flight 5191 shows that even under relatively simple conditions, making positive identifications of disaster victims is a challenge. The members of a forensic disaster team must work together to meet that challenge.

▲ Investigators study Comair Flight 5191's crumpled tail section, which was ripped from the plane before the crash, when the aircraft failed to clear the trees.

THE TEAM

Kentucky's chief medical examiner, Tracey Corey, organized the forensic response to the Flight 5191 disaster. She called upon the Kentucky Mass Disaster Team (KMDT), a group of county coroners and other experts. Planning and training sessions had prepared KMDT members for responding to a mass fatality, and within thirty to forty-five minutes after the crash, the first members of the team had arrived at the scene. The task of recovering bodies from the wreckage fell to the coroners—the Flight 5191 disaster forensics team included twenty-two of them, in addition to seven pathologists and an anthropologist.

Corey also called another member of the mass disaster team, dentistry professor Mark Bernstein of the University of Louisville. Bernstein quickly alerted four other dentists, who would share the task of examining the victims' remains, and a dental hygienist to record the exam results. After collecting a portable X-ray machine and other emergency supplies from the university campus, Bernstein headed for Frankfort, the capital of Kentucky, where the forensic work would take place.

At many disaster sites, the forensic team must work in tents or temporary shelters, but the Lexington airport is only eighteen miles from Frankfort, so the bodies from the crash site were taken to the state forensic laboratory there. Each body remained in a refrigerated truck until it could be moved into the **morgue**, a type of laboratory that is specially equipped for storing and examining bodies.

Another part of the forensic response to the Flight 5191 disaster took place in a motel in Lexington, at which the airline arranged to house victims' families. There family members, devastated by shock and grief, met with counselors who had to ask them for vital information. "Someone must sit down with forty-nine emotionally charged families and ask them detailed questions to help identification—color and length of hair, color and length of fingernails, and so forth," explained William Lee, a coroner and dentist who was

▲ Sheriff's deputies guide family members who have gathered at the airport after the crash. Disaster recovery includes family assistance and counseling.

part of the forensic team. "You need people who are trained for this."

People trained in grief and crisis counseling, sometimes called the family assistance crew, talked with families and helped the coroners gather the necessary information. The names of victims' doctors and dentists were especially important because the forensic team needed X rays and other information from the victims' records. When a body is so badly burned that it is unrecognizable, medical or dental records may be the only key to identifying it.

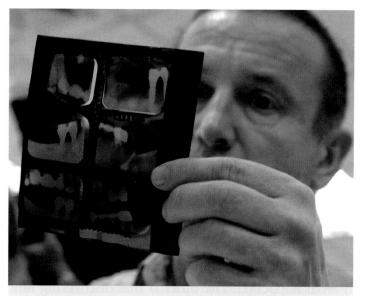

▲ Dental X rays are a highly useful tool for identifying disaster victims.

Most of the people on the plane had lived in or near Lexington, so there was little delay in getting their dental records. The plane crashed on Sunday morning, and by Tuesday, the odontological team had records for all but two of the victims.

Bernstein divided the dental records into gender groups, one for males and one for females. A member of the team then looked at each set of antemortem records, chose a distinctive feature of that person's dentition, and looked for a match among the postmortem descriptions for that gender. If the same feature appeared in more than one postmortem description, the examiner chose a second feature from the antemortem record to narrow down the match. In this way the team established matches between the antemortem and post-mortem records.

Once the bodies had been tentatively identified on the basis of one or two dental characteristics, the odontological team was ready to make positive identifications. This required a full tooth-by-tooth comparison of each victim with his or her dental records.

THE RESULTS

Forty-seven of the crash victims were identified through dental comparisons. No dental records were found for the other two victims, but one of them was identified by a fingerprint. The other had once damaged a finger and had it X-rayed. Pathologists on the disaster team matched that old X ray to the forty-ninth victim's finger bone.

After the odontological comparisons were complete, Chief Medical Examiner Corey compared the dental results with tentative identifications that had been made earlier based on the victims' descriptions, possessions, and medical records. By Wednesday evening, all victims of the crash had been positively identified. Their remains were released to their families for burial. To people who have lost family members and friends in disasters like the crash of Flight 5191, being able to claim and bury the dead can mean a great deal.

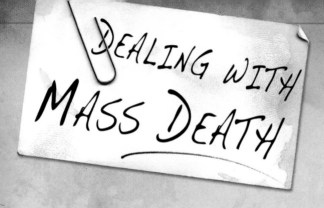

DEALING WITH MASS DEATH

THE FAMILY ASSISTANCE CREW that met with victims' relatives after the crash of Comair Flight 5191 was part of a regional group called a Disaster Mortuary Operational Response Team, or DMORT. The United States has ten DMORTs. They are part of the National Disaster Medical System, which is run by the federal Department of Health and Human Services.

When a disaster kills a large number of people, local experts and resources may be overwhelmed by the scale of the calamity. In such cases a coroner or medical examiner can ask the federal government to activate one or more DMORTs. Each region's DMORT is made up of private citizens who are pathologists, odontologists, anthropologists, fingerprint experts, and experts with other medical or forensic specialties. Most of them ordinarily work or teach, but when called into disaster duty they become temporary employees of the federal government, which pays for their services.

The primary responsibility of the DMORTs is to identify disaster victims and prepare their remains for burial. Team members perform autopsies, match teeth to dental records, and, if necessary, analyze victims' DNA and compare it with samples collected from the possessions of missing persons or from their blood relatives.

DMORTs work in whatever facilities are available near the disaster site. If the local morgue is too small or too far away, the team may set up a temporary morgue on

MEMBERS OF A *DMORT* TEAM CARRY A CORPSE FROM A
NEW ORLEANS HOUSE TWO WEEKS AFTER HURRICANE
KATRINA STRUCK THE CITY.

a military base or even in a school gym. Or it may use one of the nation's three Disaster Portable Morgue Units (DPMUs), which can be shipped anywhere by plane, train, or truck. Each DPMU contains more than ten thousand ready-to-use items, including surgical tools and exam tables, X-ray machines, and computers. In 2005, after Hurricane Katrina struck the Gulf Coast states of Louisiana and Mississippi, the federal government sent two of the DPMUs to the area, along with a thousand of the nation's 1,200 or so DMORT members.

The Katrina DMORT crews labored for months to identify the bodies of some 1,300 storm victims, as well as more than 600 sets of remains that had been washed from cemeteries by the floodwaters. It was difficult work in heartbreaking circumstances. Yet according to Katrina veteran David Senn, a forensic dentist and DMORT member from Texas, "DMORT people consider themselves strangely lucky in that they actually get to go to disaster sites and do something useful."

On the morning after a fire at the Station nightclub, the disaster team removes the body of one of the blaze's hundred victims.

CHAPTER TWO

FIRE, EARTH, AND WATER

▼ EVERY MASS DEATH IS MORE THAN

a tragedy. It is also a forensic challenge. A fire in an American nightclub and an earthquake that caused a tsunami in the Indian Ocean showed that forensic science plays an important role after both human-caused and natural disasters.

▶ THE STATION FIRE

The Station was a nightclub in West Warwick, Rhode Island. On February 20, 2003, it hosted a concert by the rock band Great White. Although the group was best known for songs released in the 1980s, the small club was full of people who had come for the performance.

To add excitement to their opening number, Great White planned a pyrotechnic (fireworks) display that would go off when the band began to play.

A cameraman was recording the performance for a local TV station's report on nightclub safety. His video camera captured what happened when Great White started their first song, at around 11 PM. The pyrotechnic display consisted of three gerbs, sparklers of a type often used in stage shows. Gerbs, which spray sparks to a distance of 15 feet, are safe when used in the proper conditions. Conditions at the Station, however, were not safe for this type of pyrotechnic show. The building

▲ Sparks from Great White's pyrotechnic display light up the stage in this image from a video that captured the start of the fire.

was constructed of flammable materials such as wood. Although by law the nightclub should have had a sprinkler system in the ceiling, this fifty-seven-year-old structure did not. The ceiling was low over the stage where the band played, and the walls on either side of the stage had been coated with foam, which was supposed to limit the amount of sound that leaked out of the building to annoy neighbors. That foam proved to be highly flammable. Sparks from the gerbs ignited the foam and started a fire. Within seconds, the walls near the stage were aflame. Smoke began to fill the room, and the fire alarm sounded.

THE CASUALTIES

The video of the disaster shows that most people in the club seemed confused at first, rather than panicked. For half a minute or so they stood and looked at the stage, perhaps thinking that the flames were part of the act. The fire moved rapidly across the ceiling, however, and people turned to flee. Although there were several exits from the club, nearly everyone tried to leave through the front door, which was separated from the main room by a passageway or corridor. People became jammed in that narrow space, struggling to push their way through, scrambling over others who had fallen to reach the door. Some clubgoers who managed to escape pulled others out to safety.

▲ Terrified clubgoers struggle to escape through the narrow doorway of the Station as smoke billows out from the fire around the stage.

One man who survived the disaster described the terrible experience this way: "People were bleeding, their hair was being burned off, their skin was just melting, skin was dangling. You could smell flesh burning even when I was inside."

Officials later estimated that more than four hundred people had been in the Station when the fire started. Of those, one hundred died. Although a few victims died in the hospital, most of the fatalities occurred at the club, particularly in the exit passageway. More than two hundred other people suffered injuries, including extensive burns in some cases.

The grim task of identifying the dead fell to the Rhode Island State Medical Examiner's office. The number of victims was so great that the medical examiner requested help from the federal government, which sent a DMORT, a Disaster Mortuary Operational Response Team, to help. The medical examiner's staff and the DMORT crew worked around the clock in the state morgue. They performed autopsies, compared dental and medical records, and gathered information from family members. By the end of the third day, all victims had been identified.

ARCHAEOLOGY IN A NEW RUIN

One member of the DMORT crew that responded to the Station fire was Richard A. Gould, a professor of anthropology at Rhode Island's Brown University. Gould had led a search for human remains in Lower Manhattan after the 9/11 terrorist attack destroyed the World Trade Center. He had also helped organize a volunteer group called Forensic Archaeology Recovery (FAR), that was based in Rhode Island.

Archaeology is the study of the human past, most often by excavating ruins and remains. FAR's purpose was to tackle disaster sites with the tools and procedures of archaeologists, who painstakingly sift through every bit of earth and record what they find. All members of FAR were professors or graduate students used to protect the evidence at the scene of a crime or disaster. Outside the hot zone was the cold zone, an area that was also fenced but did not include the site of the fire. The cold zone provided a secure parking area for emergency and official vehicles. It also featured a tent with a portable heater, where workers at the site could eat, hold meetings, and take a break from the cold.

Temperatures at the site were below freezing. The FAR group had to chip chunks of frozen ash, wood, and dirt from the ground, allow the material to thaw, and then sift it. The sifting was done at a sieving station where the volunteers passed bucketfuls of material through sieves, or screens, that rocked back and forth

▲ Debris from the site of the fire was removed to a nearby area where it could be sifted and examined. The entire area was off limits to the public.

on wooden frames. Freezing rain and an 8-inch snowfall interrupted the excavation, but as soon as the weather improved, the volunteers resumed their work.

THE CHAIN OF CUSTODY

Throughout the recovery effort, the FAR volunteers followed the forensic principle of maintaining a **chain of custody**. This principle means that everything recovered from a crime scene—or, in this case, a disaster scene—must be accounted for at all times. As soon as a piece of evidence is found, it is recorded and bagged. Every time the evidence bag changes hands, for any reason, it must be signed for by the person who takes charge of it.

If the chain of custody is broken at any point—in other words, if the identity of the person who has custody of the evidence is in doubt, even briefly—the evidence may be challenged in court, which could result in the evidence being inadmissable, or unable to be used in the case. At the scene of the Station fire, the FAR workers labeled the evidence inside a secure van, which was then used to deliver the materials to the medical examiner.

THE AFTERMATH

On March 9, more than a month after the fire, the FAR recovery effort came to an end. In addition to fragmentary

RICHARD A. GOULD has searched for human remains and possessions after several modern disasters, including the 9/11 attack on New York City and the Station nightclub fire in Rhode Island. In his 2007 book *Disaster Archaeology*, Gould describes his experiences. He also suggests principles to guide those who work to recover remains from disaster sites. Some of those principles are as follows:

• SAFETY FIRST. Disaster archaeologists must not risk their health or safety in a recovery project. A doctor or emergency medical technician should evaluate the risks of each recovery site. No team member should work alone, and team members should always look after one another.

• FOLLOW FORENSIC STANDARDS. Remember that material recovered from a disaster site may be used as evidence in a court of law. Document everything carefully and keep the chain of custody unbroken. Make sure that everything removed from the site is fully accounted for at all times.

• ARCHAEOLOGY SPEAKS FOR THE VICTIMS. Keep in mind that by recovering victims' remains and belongings, disaster archaeologists help the courts and the victims' families better understand what happened and how people died. The recovery has a compassionate purpose as well. It can bring some measure of comfort to grieving family members, friends, and communities.

such as teddy bears. Flowers piled up. After the fence came down and the site was bulldozed, family members and townspeople acting on their own created new memorials on the vacant lot, which served as the setting for unofficial remembrance ceremonies.

▶ AN INDIAN OCEAN DISASTER

The longest earthquake ever recorded by modern instruments shook the floor of the Indian Ocean for more than eight minutes on December 26, 2004, and tore an 800-mile rift in the ocean floor. The quake measured between 9.1 and 9.3 on the Richter scale, the scientific basis for classifying the size of earth movments. (For comparison, the 1988 Loma Prieta earthquake, which caused serious damage along the central California coast, measured between 6.9 and 7.1 on the scale, and the February 2010 earthquake in the South American nation of Chile measured 8.8.)

FROM QUAKE TO WAVE

All over the world, scientific instruments recorded the quake in the Indian Ocean, known as the Sumatran-Andaman earthquake because it happened between the island of Sumatra, which is part of the nation of Indonesia, and the Andaman Islands group. Earth scientist Charles Ammon of Penn State University said, "Globally, this earthquake was large enough to basically vibrate the whole planet as much as half an inch, or a centimeter."

But the planet-shaking quake was just the beginning of this modern disaster. Earth movements caused a section of the ocean floor to rise suddenly several yards, or meters, then fall back down. The water above the part of the ocean floor that rose was suddenly raised, too, and this sent a wave outward in all directions. In the deep waters of the ocean's center, the wave traveled very fast and was only 2 feet (less than a meter) high. But as the wave reached shallower water near shore, it slowed down and gained height. By the time it struck the coast of Aceh, the northernmost part of Sumatra, the wave was enormous: between 79 and 100 feet (24 and 30 meters) high.

When such a wave strikes land, it is called a tsunami—and it can be deadly. The Indian Ocean tsunami came ashore on coastlines all around the rim of the ocean. Because many of those coastal regions were densely populated, the effect was devastating. Thousands of people were battered or drowned when the great wave crashed down upon them. Others were swept helplessly out to sea as the waters withdrew with a rush. Entire villages and towns were destroyed, while roads and services such as electricity and water were wiped out across large areas.

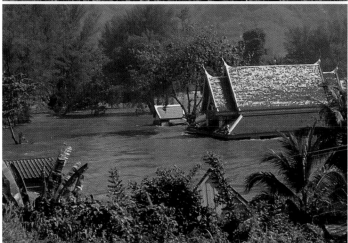

▲ Waves surge high around a temple in Phuket, Thailand—
part of the aftermath of a severe earthquake under the
floor of the Indian Ocean.

THE DEATH TOLL

The United Nations estimates that deaths from the tsunami totaled about 230,000 people in eleven countries. Another 125,000 were injured, nearly 46,000 were missing, and more than 1.5 million were displaced from their homes. The hardest-hit countries were Indonesia (especially northern Sumatra), Sri Lanka (an island nation south of India), India, and Thailand.

Images of destruction filled the news. So did reports of the suffering caused by the tsunami, along with stories of survival and heroism. Governments and aid agencies around the world poured relief into the stricken area in the form of money, supplies, and workers. Among the workers were pathologists, DNA technicians, and other forensic specialists. They came from many nations to help the police, pathologists, and other officials in the stricken countries identify the dead. In Thailand alone, the disaster-victim identification (DVI) team consisted of three hundred people from thirty countries.

▲ A citizen of southern India sits atop the wreckage of his home. The tsunami displaced a million and half people.

A FORENSIC CHALLENGE

Victim identification after the Indian Ocean tsunami was the biggest challenge ever faced by forensic science—not only because of the sheer number of victims, but also because the disaster site was spread across a large area of the planet. To complicate matters, there was widespread damage to roads and communication systems. For weeks after the disaster, just getting food and fresh water to desperate survivors in remote areas such as Aceh was a major challenge.

Another complication was the lack of official records for many of the villagers, fishing people, and others who were lost. It was impossible to name all the dead, or figure out exactly who was missing, without a complete and accurate population list to begin with. Many thousands of family members and friends begged recovery workers to find their loved ones, but in all too many cases entire families and communities were gone, leaving no one to ask for the dead, or identify the bodies that were recovered.

Many of the better-documented victims were tourists from Europe, the United States, Australia, and South Africa who had been vacationing in the region, especially at popular beach resorts in Thailand. For both foreigners and local people who were missing and feared dead after the tsunami, authorities began the difficult and time-consuming process of gathering information and material that could link an identity to one of the thousands of bodies left in the disaster's wake. Dental and medical records, physical descriptions, fingerprints if they were available, personal items such as toothbrushes that might yield DNA samples, or DNA samples from relatives—any of these things, if available, might identify a victim.

Forensic specialists had to battle time and the natural processes of decay, too. The disaster had occurred in a tropical region, with high heat and humidity that led to rapid **decomposition** of the human remains. In some of the hardest-hit areas, where there was no electricity for refrigeration, authorities or local people temporarily buried the dead in mass graves. This was partly to prevent the spread of disease and partly to slow decomposition so that the remains could later be identified. Other bodies washed ashore or were recovered at sea weeks or even months after the tsunami. By the time the DVI teams saw some bodies, the remains were so badly decomposed or damaged that there were no easily recognizable physical features. In some cases it was impossible to tell the person's gender or ethnic background without a detailed examination.

RECOVERING THE REMAINS

Each country, and sometimes separate areas within a country, organized the process of victim identification

▲ In Indonesia's hard-hit Aceh province, a grandmother looks at pictures of missing children. Photos, posters, and pleas for information were everywhere after the tsunami.

in its own way, depending upon its resources and customs. The general pattern, though, was much the same everywhere. The first step was recovery of the bodies. Crews of volunteers, often led by police or other local authorities, collected remains from beaches, hillsides, the rubble of smashed buildings, and the places where bodies had been stored or buried.

Recovered bodies were brought to processing centers. Morgues and labs served as processing centers, but many other centers were set up in whatever buildings were available. Near the beach resorts in Thailand, for example, Buddhist temples came into

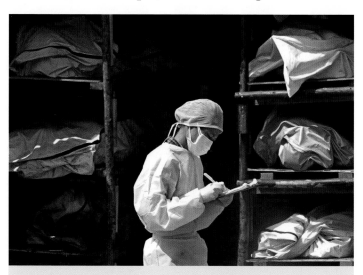

▲ A wat, or temple, in southern Thailand became a temporary morgue for the bodies of Thais and foreign vacationers killed by the great wave.

service as temporary morgues. Dry ice was trucked in to cool the morgues. Bodies were stored in refrigerated shipping containers.

Large numbers of people came to the morgues to search for the remains of their loved ones. Pictures of the missing were everywhere, with signs offering rewards for information. Recovery workers were besieged by men and women who showed them photos and begged them to search for the people in the pictures. Amid all this suffering and confusion, the forensic technicians—including dentists, pathologists, anthropologists, and others—put on protective clothing and masks and went to work.

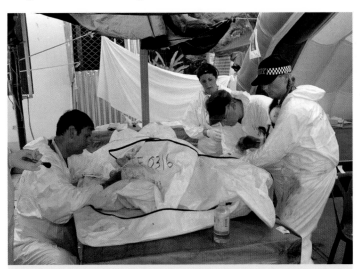

▲ A British forensic team works to identify bodies at another temple-turned-morgue in Thailand. Professionals from seventeen nations served at this site.

▲ An unidentified foreign tsunami victim is buried in Sri Lanka. DNA samples and burial records were kept for the unknown victims, in the hope that they may one day be identified.

Thai authorities received a lot of forensic assistance, including equipment, technicians, and money for DNA typing.

Before the disaster Thailand's infrastructure—the country's operational framework, which includes roads, electrical service, and medical and forensic systems—was more advanced than those in the other countries hit by the tsunami. Although the tsunami struck many of Thailand's islands and coastal towns, most of the infrastructure was unharmed, and this helped with the recovery and identification of bodies. Heavily hit Aceh, in contrast, was difficult to reach even before the tsunami. One result of the 2004 tsunami, however, was that Indonesia and other countries in the region recognized the need to develop better plans for disaster response, including recovering and identifying victims.

Years after the Indian Ocean tsunami, questions remained unanswered. Some bodies were never identified. Thousands of other victims could not be officially pronounced dead because they were lost at sea and their bodies were never recovered. Against the destructive power of one of nature's mightiest forces, human efforts—even our most advanced scientific techniques—have limits.

Three years before the tsunami, a human-caused disaster had also pushed forensic science to its limits. In 2001 terrorists crashed a plane into a Pennsylvania field, destroyed part of the largest military office building in the United States, and turned 16 acres of New York City into a huge crime scene.

On the night of September 11, 2001, part of the Pentagon lay in ruins. Firefighters searched the dangerous site for survivors.

CHAPTER THREE

DELIBERATE DISASTER

▼ EARTHQUAKES ARE NATURAL DISASTERS.

Nightclub fires are tragic accidents. But some disasters are the result of deliberate acts that were intended to hurt as many people as possible. Large-scale terrorist attacks have killed more people and destroyed more property than some natural disasters.

The modern world has seen too many such attacks. In 1988 a bomb blew up Pan Am Flight 103, killing all 259 people aboard the plane, as well as eleven who died when the wreckage rained down on the town of Lockerbie, Scotland. In 2002 suicide bombers set off several explosions in a nightclub in Bali, Indonesia, killing more than 200 people and injuring 240. In 2004 ten bombs on four commuter trains in Madrid, Spain, killed nearly 200 people and injured as many as 1,800. After each disaster, forensic science helped authorities investigate the crime and identify the victims.

The 9/11 attack on the United States in 2001 killed nearly 3,000 people, including the terrorists themselves, at three separate sites. This shocking event, one of the worst disasters in American history, led to the largest forensic investigation the country had ever seen. Engineers and explosives experts probed mountains of wreckage to discover exactly how the tragedy had happened. Medical forensic teams, meanwhile, began the grim task of identifying the victims' remains.

▶ THE 9/11 ATTACK

On the morning of September 11, 2001, nineteen hijackers seized control of four commercial aircraft that had taken off from East Coast airports, bound for Los Angeles or San Francisco. The hijackers flew one of the planes into the North Tower of the World Trade Center in New York City, one into the South Tower, and a third into the Pentagon, the huge military office building in Washington, D.C. The fourth plane's hijackers may have planned to fly it into the Capitol building in Washington, but it crashed near Shanksville, Pennsylvania, after some of the passengers struggled with the hijackers.

▲ The north tower of the World Trade Center is already burning as a hijacked airliner approaches the south tower (upper left). The plane then strikes the tower, igniting a fireball of jet fuel and sending black smoke billowing high above New York.

The crashes in New York and Washington produced great destruction and created panic and confusion, but worse was to come. The aircraft, loaded with enough fuel to fly across the country, set off very hot fires high in the two stricken office towers of the WTC. Less than an hour after impact, the South Tower collapsed. The North Tower lasted a little more than 100 minutes

WHEN THEY WERE COMPLETED in 1970 and 1971, the two towers of the World Trade Center in New York City became the tallest features of the city's skyline. To enemies of the United States, they were a tempting target.

On February 26, 1993, an explosion rocked the underground public parking garage beneath the WTC. The blast blew a 20,000-square-foot hole through several levels of the garage and sent thick smoke billowing up through the stairwells of both towers. It also knocked out electrical power to the World Trade Center. Hundreds of people were trapped in the elevators.

Emergency vehicles poured into the area. As rescue workers helped dazed survivors evacuate the buildings, police officers, FBI agents, and bomb technicians investigated the explosion. After making sure that there were no more bombs waiting to explode, they gathered traces of the explosive material and measured the size of the blast damage.

The core of the bomb was an explosive made from urea nitrate, a chemical used as lawn and crop fertilizer. Metal particles had been packed around the explosive to increase the damage, along with tanks of hydrogen, a flammable gas that would create a fireball. The whole thing had weighed about 1,500 pounds and must have been delivered to the garage in a vehicle. A long fuse had ignited the bomb, giving the bombers time to get away.

Bomb technicians located pieces of vehicles in the wreckage at the blast site. A vehicle identification number

A 1993 TERRORIST ATTACK ON THE WORLD TRADE CENTER LEFT A BOMB CRATER IN THE STRUCTURE'S PARKING GARAGE.

found on a piece of an axle belonged to a van owned by a rental company in New Jersey. Security cameras at the World Trade Center showed that van entering the parking garage before the explosion. The van had been rented by a man named Mohammed Salameh, who told the rental company that the vehicle had been stolen. Federal agents staked out the rental office, and when Salameh showed up to collect the money he had paid as a security deposit on the van, he was arrested. Authorities later arrested his five fellow conspirators, all with ties to radical Islamic groups such as Al-Qaeda. All are now serving life sentences in U.S. prisons.

Six people died in the 1993 car-bombing of the World Trade Center, and more than a thousand were injured. Yet the damage could have been much worse. The terrorists wanted the bomb to destroy the foundation supports in one corner of the North Tower, which would cause the tower to collapse and knock down the South Tower. This did not happen. The blast traveled through the concrete flooring of the parking garage but failed to destroy the stronger steel-reinforced supports. It would be another eight years before the world would see the terrible sight of the two towers falling.

▲ Hundreds of people joined the rescue and recovery efforts, risking their own lives and health to remove victims and their remains from the rubble of the World Trade Center.

All human remains were carefully carried from the site, draped with American flags. Every bucketful of loose debris was sifted for bone fragments or personal items that might help identify victims. Debris was then loaded into dump trucks and hauled to landfills and salvage yards, where it was again searched and sorted into categories. Some of the steel was saved for use in memorials.

THE FALL OF THE TOWERS

Federal agents had quickly discovered the names of the hijackers, and reconstructing the events leading up to the attack had not been difficult. But investigators from the National Institute of Standards and Technology (NIST), the federal agency that investigates disasters such as the collapse of a building or a bridge, wanted to know what had made the towers fall. At Ground Zero and the salvage yards, as well as in NIST laboratories, experts in structural engineering, metallurgy, and chemistry performed a kind of "building autopsy," examining pieces of the steel from the WTC buildings for signs of the effects of heat, chemical reactions, or pressure.

The NIST reported the results of its forensic examination of the WTC wreckage in 2005. The report included the following key points.

- The impacts of the large, fast-moving planes destroyed some of the towers'

▲ Investigators search the crash site near Shanksville, Pennsylvania, for traces of the crashed aircraft's passengers and crew, or of the terrorists who hijacked it.

everyone in the plane. For weeks, volunteers searched the surrounding landscape, even climbing into trees to look for body parts. Eventually they collected 1,500 scorched fragments. DNA tests or, in a few cases, fingerprints linked each of the thirty-three passengers and seven crew members aboard the plane to at least one of these fragments.

THE PENTAGON

Victim identification at the Pentagon was nearly as successful as in Pennsylvania. Remains from the

▲ Soldiers from the National Guard patrol the disaster scene at the Pentagon. Bodies and body parts from this site were taken to a temporary morgue for identification.

Pentagon disaster site were brought to a temporary morgue in an aircraft hangar on an Air Force base not far from the nation's capital. One of the specialists who served there was forensic anthropologist Robert Mann, who had years of experience identifying the remains of American service people who had been lost on military duty. In his 2006 book *Forensic Detective*, Mann described the morgue's operating system.

As bodies or body parts arrived, each was given an identifying number and X-rayed. This first X-ray image was not a step toward identification—it was a precaution to determine whether there were any dangerous items such as knives, guns, razors, or explosives on the body. This step was necessary because any given corpse could be that of a Pentagon security officer or a terrorist. Once cleared by a negative X ray, bodies were moved to the triage station.

Normally the term "triage" applies to emergency or battlefield settings, where injured people are sorted into three groups: those to be sent to a hospital, those whose condition is less serious, and those who are beyond help. In terms of victim identification, triage means deciding what step came next for each set of remains, depending on its condition. If the hands had been recovered, for example, the body would be fingerprinted by an FBI agent. (Fingerprints were especially helpful in identifying the Pentagon fatalities because many of the victims were military people whose prints were on file.). Jaws, teeth, and bones were X-rayed for comparison with antemortem dental and medical records. Personal effects such as clothes, jewelry, toys, and umbrellas were stored in an evidence room. Later, if they could be linked to a particular victim, they would be returned to that person's family.

"Two distinct environments, one stationary and one moving at more than five hundred miles an hour, had collided," Mann wrote about the crash into the Pentagon. "[T]he result was a mass of tangled debris, human remains, broken hearts, and agonizing memories." Sifting through the debris, recovery workers made strange finds—half-melted telephones and unburned file folders amid piles of ash. "There were even a few dried-out old chicken bones," Mann reported. "They were very dry and dark, unlike bones recently discarded." He thought they were "the remains of a worker's lunch discarded during construction of the Pentagon in 1943." The chicken bones probably lay quietly out of sight in a floor, wall, or ceiling for more than half a century, until disaster struck.

Many of the Pentagon disaster identifications were made through DNA. The Armed Forces Institute of Pathology performed the DNA typing, which took months to complete. In the end, the experts had identified remains belonging to all but five victims of the disaster. Although the identities of the five were known—they were a child who had been on the plane, and four adults who had been in the Pentagon—none of their remains were ever found.

THE WORLD TRADE CENTER

New York's temporary 9/11 disaster morgue was also an aircraft hangar, at LaGuardia Airport on Long Island. The city's medical examiner realized at once that DNA typing would be vital to identifying those who had died at the World Trade Center. Many of the victims had been crushed, fragmented, and burned—they could not be identified in any other way.

On September 12, spouses and other family members of missing people began lining up at a family crisis center staffed by city employees and DMORT members. They gave detailed descriptions of their missing loved ones and offered hairbrushes or toothbrushes that might yield DNA samples. Parents, children, and siblings of missing people gave samples of their own DNA to be used in kinship matching against remains from the site.

Officials in New York promised the grieving families that every tiny bit of human material recovered from the site would be tested. The city's forensic DNA lab was not equal to the task of performing hundreds of thousands, perhaps millions, of tests, even though it was the largest such lab in the United States. The city hired several commercial DNA testing labs to help meet the challenge.

A total of 293 fairly intact corpses were recovered from the WTC wreckage. Most of them came to light in the first few weeks. Around 20,000 body parts or fragments of bone or tissue were recovered from the site in the months after the attack, and as late as 2006 pieces of bone were still being discovered on the rooftops of buildings near the disaster zone.

▲ Two days after the terrorist attack, these men fear the worst. Their friend was employed by a company whose World Trade Center offices were destroyed in the attack.

On the first anniversary of the attack, 1,481 victims had been identified by X rays, photographs, finger-prints, or some other method. More than half of the identifications were based on DNA evidence alone.

From that point on, all hopes for further identifi-cation rested with DNA typing. Many of the remains, however, were too small or too degraded by fire to pro-duce usable DNA sequences. By the end of 2002 the medical examiner's office had reached the limits of

▲ Charles S. Hirsch, New York's chief medical examiner,
oversaw the massive WTC victim-identification project.
New DNA techniques used by his team were later applied
to tsunami victims.

standard DNA technology. Refusing to give up, chief medical officer Charles S. Hirsch and his staff spent two more years and millions of dollars to apply two new DNA sequencing techniques that had been developed in research labs but never tried in the field.

One of these techniques is called mini short tandem repeats. The other is termed single nucleotide polymorphism analysis. Both approaches can be used on pieces of DNA strands smaller than the size required for standard tests. The result was 111 more identifications. After this successful application in New York, the new techniques came into use for later DVI operations, including the Indian Ocean tsunami.

By the spring of 2005, however, even the new techniques could produce no more results in the WTC case. With a total of 1,592 official identifications, the medical examiner declared New York's DVI effort at an end. Thousands of unidentified human remains from the World Trade Center, however, are still in storage. Advances in DNA technology may soon make it possible to sequence and identify those fragments, because forensic science is changing and growing rapidly. It is an ever more powerful tool to help us cope with the unpredictable, uncontrollable events that we call disasters.

▼ GLOSSARY

antemortem before death

anthropology the study of human beings past and
present, with emphasis on the differences among
groups

anthropometry measuring the human body; the
measurements obtained from a great many
bodies, called anthropometrics, have produced
valuable databases

archaeology the investigation of past cultures and
societies, usually by excavating ancient ruins and
studying the objects or human remains
discovered there

autopsy a medical examination performed on a body
to find the cause of death; a forensic autopsy also
tries to establish the time and manner of death

chain of custody the record of the history of each
piece of evidence, to show who has had control of
the evidence at each moment from the time it is
collected to the time it is used in a trial or
disposed of in some other way

coroner a public official responsible for determining
cause of death; the position does not require
medical training

decomposition the process of decay and tissue
breakdown that happens after death as a result of
the action of bacteria

disaster a sudden or relatively rapid event that causes large-scale death, injury, and/or property damage; may be natural or caused by human actions

DMORT (Disaster Mortuary Operational Response Team) in the United States, one of ten groups of experts who help with forensics and victim identification after disasters; administered by the federal government

DNA deoxyribonucleic acid, the substance that contains each individual's genetic code and is found in blood, saliva, and other tissues from the body

DNA typing the use of DNA to identify individuals; DNA testing may also match a person to a piece of evidence or establish a relationship between two individuals

fatalities deaths

forensic science the use of scientific knowledge or methods to investigate crimes, identify suspects, and try criminal cases in court

forensics in general, debate or review of any question of fact relating to the law; often used to refer to forensic science

homicide murder

medical examiner (ME) a public official responsible for determining cause of death; the position requires medical training

metallurgy the science of metals, especially their structure and their behavior under various conditions

morgue a special medical facility, usually part of a hospital or forensic lab, where bodies are stored and where autopsies are performed

odontology the study of teeth and dental work; forensic odontology is the use of teeth to identify the dead

pathologist physician who specializes in the study of illness and death, especially in determining the cause of death

postmortem after death

▼ FIND OUT MORE

FURTHER READING

Adams, Bradley J. *Forensic Anthropology.* New York: Chelsea House, 2006.

Denega, Danielle. *Skulls and Skeletons: True-Life Stories of Bone Detectives.* New York: Franklin Watts, 2007.

Funkhluser, John. *Forensic Science for High School Students.* Dubuque, IA: Kendall Hunt, 2005.

Shone, Rob. *Corpses and Skeletons: The Science of Forensic Anthropology.* New York: Rosen, 2008.

Thomas, Peggy. *Forensic Anthropology: The Growing Science of Talking Bones.* Rev. ed. New York: Facts On File, 2003.

WEBSITES

www.hhs.gov/aspr/opeo/ndms/index.html

www.hhs.gov/aspr/opeo/ndms/teams/dmort.html
The websites of the federal government's National Disaster Medical System (NDMS) and Disaster Mortuary Operational Response Teams (DMORT) give overviews of how these agencies provide medical and forensic aid after disasters or terrorist attacks.

www.disasters.org/dera/disasters.htm
The Disaster Preparedness and Emergency Response

Association is made up of volunteers who help law enforcement and government agencies with the process of disaster recovery in many countries.

http://wtc.nist.gov/pubs/factsheets/faqs_8_2006.htm
The National Institute of Standards and Technology answers questions about the World Trade Center collapse at this site.

www.aafs.org/yfsf/index.htm
The website of the American Academy of Forensic Sciences features the Young Forensic Scientists Forum, with information on careers in forensics. The site also links to other Internet resources.

www.crimezzz.net/forensic_history/index.htm
The Crimeline page offers a brief timeline of developments in forensic science from prehistory to the present.

www.forensicmag.com
Forensic Magazine's web page features case studies and news about developments in forensic science, including articles about recovery and investigation work after major disasters.

▼ BIBLIOGRAPHY

The author found these books and articles especially
helpful when researching this volume.

Bass, Bill, and Jon Jefferson. *Beyond the Body Farm.*
New York: Morrow, 2007.

Dotinga, Randy. "Tsunami Tests Limits of
Forensics."*Wired,* January 6, 2005, online at
www.wired.com/medtech/health/news/2005/01/66
184?currentPage=all

Dunlap, David. "Expert Supports Search Methods for
9/11 Remains at Bank Building." *New York Times,*
August 26, 2006.

Ferllini, Roxana. *Silent Witness.* Buffalo, NY: Firefly
Books, 2002.

Foote, Kenneth E. *Shadowed Ground: America's
Landscapes of Violence and Tragedy.* 2nd edition.
Austin: University of Texas Press, 2003.

"Forensic Dentistry Key in Identifying Victims of
Tsunamis, Other Disasters." *Science Daily,* April 6,
2005, online at www.sciencedaily.com/releases/
2005/03/050326005336.htm

Gould, Richard A. *Disaster Archaeology.* Salt Lake
City: University of Utah Press, 2007.

Hunter, John, and Margaret Cox. *Forensic
Archaeology: Advances in Theory and Practice.*
London and New York: Routledge, 2005.

Klepinger, Linda L. *Fundamentals of Forensic Anthropology.* Hoboken, NJ: Wiley, 2006.

Langwiesche, William. *American Ground: Unbuilding the World Trade Center.* New York: Farrar, Straus, and Giroux, 2002.

Linenthal, Ed. *The Unfinished Bombing: Oklahoma City in American Memory.* New York: Oxford University Press, 2001.

Lipton, Eric. "At Limits of Science, 9/11 ID Effort Comes to an End." *New York Times,* April 3, 2005, 34.

Mann, Robert. *Forensic Detective.* New York: Ballantine, 2006.

Marshall, Andrew. "Forensics: How to ID the Bodies." *Time,* January 10, 2005, online at www.time.com/time/magazine/article/0,9171,1015889,00.html

Nafte, Myriam. *Flesh and Bone: An Introduction to Forensic Anthropology.* Durham, NC: Carolina Academic Press, 2000.

National Commission on Terrorist Attacks on the United States. "The 9/11 Commission Report: Executive Summary." July 22, 2004. Online at http://govinfo.library.unt.edu/911/report/911Report_Exec.pdf

Oxenham, Marc, editor. *Forensic Approaches to Death, Disaster, and Abuse.* Bowen Hills: Australian Academic Press, 2008.

Page, Douglas. "Forensic Disaster Response: The Crash of Comair 5191." *Forensic Magazine*, February/March 2007, online at www.forensicmag.com/articles.asp?pid=129

———. "Life in a Disaster Morgue." *Forensic Magazine*, December 2005/January 2006, online at www.forensicmag.com/articles.asp?pid=68

Shaler, Robert. *Who They Were: Inside the World Trade Center Story*. New York: Free Press, 2005.

Walton, Marsha. "Scientists: Sumatra quake longest ever recorded." *CNN.com*, May 20, 2005, online at http://edition.cnn.com/2005/TECH/science/05/19/sumatra.quake/index.html

▼ INDEX

▼ ABOUT THE AUTHOR

REBECCA STEFOFF is the author of many books on scientific subjects for young readers. In addition to writing previous volumes in the Forensic Science Investigated series, she has explored the world of evolutionary biology in Marshall Cavendish's Family Trees series; she also wrote *Robot* and *Camera* for Marshall Cavendish's Great Inventions series. After publishing *Charles Darwin and the Evolution Revolution* (Oxford University Press, 1996), she appeared in the *A&E Biography* program on Darwin and his work. Stefoff lives in Portland, Oregon. You can learn more about her books for young readers at **www.rebeccastefoff.com**.